PASSAGE BY PASSAGE
A GOSPEL JOURNEY

PASSAGE
BY
PASSAGE

A GOSPEL JOURNEY

REVISED COMMON LECTIONARY
YEAR A

KAYLA MCCLURG

Washington, DC

Cover and book design by Martin Saunders

Cover photograph by Dan Brady
© 2003 Dan Brady
http://www.flickr.com/photos/djbrady

First Edition

inward/outward
The Church of the Saviour
1640 Columbia Road NW
Washington DC 20009

inwardoutwardeditor@gmail.com
www.inwardoutward.org

ISBN 978-0-9894000-1-5

*For all who prayerfully
labor week by week,
searching scripture for a
coin, a question, a light.
You do not search alone.*

CONTENTS

LENT

EASTER & PENTECOST

Ordinary Time

Introduction

One of my lifelong soul friendships began when I was eight years old. In the middle of an otherwise normal school day, the teacher asked me to walk a girl home whom I didn't know very well. This most unfortunate third grader had just thrown up on the classroom floor, the ultimate social faux pas, and I was one of the few kids who did not laugh. Remarkable gifts come disguised this way, in the homeliest of encounters. Ordinary moments, embarrassing even, have awesome potential for one's future.

With her head hanging low as we walked across the schoolyard, she said, "You probably hate having to do this." I said, "No, it's okay. You couldn't help it." That's all. Nothing remarkable. We just trudged along, silently, and never mentioned it again.

Nor did we forget. Both of us still recall that encounter as the pivotal moment when we went from being two anonymous kids in the classroom to friends who continue to walk beside each other through life's varied messes.

This is the good news: We are embarrassingly human, but we are not alone. Together we are able to face whatever happens. We get to walk each other home.

When I read the Gospel, I sense this sort of companionship. I read not only to learn about God's movement in human history but to see, in these stories, the stories of my own life and our life together in community. I read it to experience Jesus and all those he encountered as coming alongside and "walking us home."

In their tales of distress, I experience our own distress. In their isolation and fear, or in their reckless boldness, I see our own. When they turn to follow the way of life, and when they turn away, I see our own tendency to wander and return. In these stories I see what an absolute mess we can be, embarrassingly human. I see how far we still live from compassion. And I find hope in the radical mercy that waits for us along the way. I sense the embrace of a love that has no end.

These reflections on the Gospel lessons of the Revised Common Lectionary are written not by a learned theologian but simply another pilgrim on the way. I do not know what these remarkable stories "really mean" any more than I know what you or I "really mean." I likely have missed the mark at many junctures, and I urge you to refer to other sources for fuller understanding. All I have to offer are a few random thoughts to jumpstart your own.

One thing I do know about the Gospel is that it is for all of us. It is a wide field where all of God's children are invited to play and to ponder life's biggest questions. Doubt is welcome here. Seeing things another way is welcome here. May this little book spark your own surprises and questions and discoveries. In the One Story, may we all uncover more of our own.

- Kayla McClurg

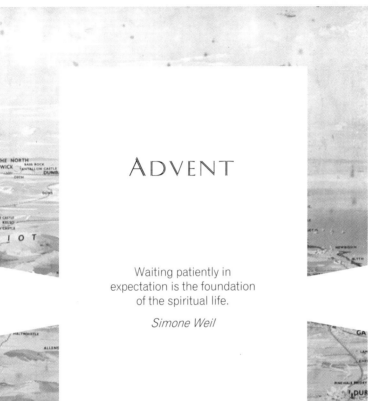

ADVENT

Waiting patiently in
expectation is the foundation
of the spiritual life.

Simone Weil

ARE WE READY?

Matthew 24:36-44

Be ready all the time.
For the Son of Man will
come when least expected.

The thought of Jesus sneaking up on us at some unknown hour does not sound like the best kind of news. Considering the stress we already are under, now we have to guard against this, too? Constantly at red level alert, under the threat of invasion, even by Jesus whom we profess to love, sounds utterly exhausting. The adrenaline pumps just thinking about it. Maybe he could give us a call or send a text first?

Really, does it seem likely to you that Jesus wants to scare us into readiness? He is not some evil engineer stepping off the train as it races forward at top speed, leaving us to steer the thing, then threatening punishment if we get off track. He is the Jesus who said things like, "I am with you to the ends of the earth." Maybe his dire warnings are not about some future unexpected day; maybe they are about *all* our days.

To be on guard against some spectacular, sky-breaking day, date unknown, leaves me feeling anxious and unprepared. To know that he comes unexpectedly *every day* changes my life. Now each situation, each place, each person is where Jesus is apt to appear. Life becomes less of a threat and more of an adventure. Jesus showing up again—maybe today!—becomes the expectation that he will, no doubt, show up today. Will I notice him, again and again? Will I be ready?

Open my eyes to see you.
Every day, surprise me.

Turn From Your Sin

Matthew 3:1-12

*Prove by the way
you live that you
have really turned.*

Before the people even had encountered Jesus, John was preaching that they must turn from their sins. Turning was the way *to* God, not what they would get busy working on afterward. I have heard it more frequently taught that first we "come to Jesus"—have some sort of breakthrough experience of God in our life—and then we take inventory, name the sins that bind us and begin to change our lives. John reverses the process, saying first we will turn from our sin—walk another way—and *then* we will turn to God.

Maybe I'm splitting a camel's hair of difference, but John's way urges me to take responsibility. Everything that has separated me from God, I don't just pray out of my life; I live my way into another way. I put on my hiking boots and start climbing the mountain of a different kind of life, which prepares me for the One who will baptize me into the depths of the new.

If I "come to Jesus" and then wait for him to get my act together for me, I run the risk of seeing sin as a psychological dilemma, not tied to the choices I make every day. "Guard my heart," I earnestly pray, but my finances and my daily schedule? I'll watch over those. I can give mental assent to new life but never get to the life-changing turn. The turn signal might keep clicking my good intentions, but this does not mean I have actually turned.

*Show me how I still need to
turn and walk another way.*

SHOW SOME RESPECT

Matthew 11:2-11

Were you looking for
a prophet? John is
more than a prophet.

Jesus and John first "meet" in their mother's wombs, when Mary's cousin Elizabeth welcomes her into the refuge of her home. Elizabeth is in the sixth month of her own surprising pregnancy, having thought she was barren. Her unborn child, John, leaps in response to Mary's greeting, somersaulting with excitement to have a visit from his yet-to-be-born cousin, Jesus.

Did they play together as children? ("You can be the Messiah this time." "No, you! I was Messiah last time; it's your turn."). But we do know they loved each other as adults. It could have been otherwise. John had his own disciples, just like Jesus. He had his own creeds and disciplines and way of being in community. Yet they do not compete for leadership or follower-ship. They both stay true to their own callings and honor the other in his. When we think of the competition among churches today, their brotherly support is remarkable.

Each of them is fully and humbly devoted to a vision beyond human capacity, calling them to sacrifice and, eventually, death. They are servants of a realm they can see clearly yet cannot express completely. John says of Jesus, "I am unworthy even to untie his sandals." Jesus says of John, "Among all who have ever lived, none is greater than he." Is not this a love worth emulating? This kind of mutual love and respect could change the world.

Thank you, Jesus and John, for your
devotion to God, and each other.

The Wisdom of Sleep

Matthew 1:18-25

As he considered
breaking the engagement,
he fell asleep.

Sometimes the best response to a difficult situation is to sleep on it. Joseph, thinking it might save Mary from public disgrace to break their engagement quietly, nearly derails God's plans. Fortunately, he does what wise folks do—Joseph takes a nap. As he dozes, a dream tells him not to be afraid to marry but to step up boldly and claim his unconventional family. His fatherly faithfulness from that point forward is of epic proportion.

Is it too simplistic to suggest that sleep is a key component of faithful discipleship? Many of us are adrenaline-addicted junkies, as though only productivity and busyness will prove our love. Sleeping certainly will not right the wrongs of the world. Sleeping does not feed the hungry or free the prisoner or clothe the naked. And so we keep on. Weariness wages war within us. Enveloped in a weary fog, we risk missing much of the beauty and creativity, the spontaneity, the life within life.

When we do admit we need rest, we then are apt to search for retreats and meditation classes and support groups and books, all good, but all adding to our busy state. We get up extra early to pray without going to bed early the night before, and we wonder why inner peace is in short supply. Joseph's intuition knew what he would need for the road ahead. Perhaps we, too, would be well served by simply...falling...asleep.

Will you be able to manage things for me,
God, if I bow out and get some sleep?

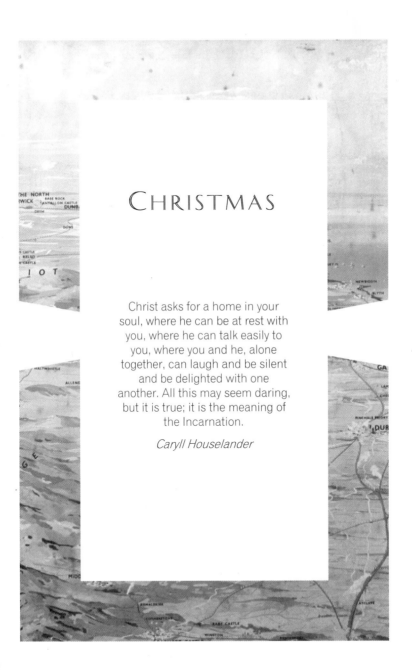

CHRISTMAS

Christ asks for a home in your soul, where he can be at rest with you, where he can talk easily to you, where you and he, alone together, can laugh and be silent and be delighted with one another. All this may seem daring, but it is true; it is the meaning of the Incarnation.

Caryll Houselander

Taking Our Lives Seriously

Matthew 2:13-23

An angel appeared to
Joseph in another dream, warning
him to leave immediately.

Joseph's advanced practice in the spiritual discipline of rest gives him opportunity for three more dreams to guide him and his family through some of the weightiest decisions of their lives. The guidance he receives in these dreams is not only spiritual, but geographical, calling him to new degrees of trust by calling him and his family to new places. "Escape to Egypt," one of the dreams says. "Go back to Israel," says another. "Go instead to Galilee," says another. A man with a young wife and newborn child surely would prefer to settle down, not become rootless refugees, but Joseph and Mary do not demand the comforts of home. When they are called, they go, not seeking safety at the expense of obedience.

Joseph and Mary's faithfulness is a model of what it looks like to take our lives seriously, to live as though what we do matters, as though we serve a higher purpose than our own good pleasure. Each of our choices, each prayerful decision, is not without consequence. Our choices impact us, as well as those in the immediate circle around us, and others we will never even know. Our decisions to follow, or not to follow, the scraps of guidance we receive, expand in ever-widening circles, affecting the world around us and beyond us. This story is not only Joseph and Mary's family story. It is ours. We, too, must choose well.

Guide me, in my waking and in my sleeping.
May even my small obediences be used for you.

THE ETERNAL WORD

John 1:1-18

*The Word became
human and lived right
here among us.*

The nature of the Word is reconciliation and all-encompassing love. If this is true, I assume it describes the state of things in any neighborhood where disciples of the Word live, right? *Right?*

One Sunday, after another thought-provoking time with one of the communities pondering this Word, I passed by a woman who was sitting on the sidewalk asking for money. She asked politely, which was curious because she was well-known in our neighborhood as someone more apt to yell vulgarities at people passing by. Intrigued, I stopped. Maybe today will be a turning point for both of us, I thought. Maybe true connection—real communion—is possible. How lovely it will be.

As soon as I tried to talk with her, however, she flew into a rage, screaming, "Rich white bitch! F- - - you, bitch!" I scowled and went home, defeated.

What does it mean, that the Word became flesh, one of us, all of us? Do we see him now in all his "distressing disguises"—rich and poor; ashamed and proud; addicted and in recovery; in prison and on the streets; inside the church and walking away? He has few who care, fewer still who will listen. It is not easy to live in and by and for this Word spoken into existence on behalf of us all, yet never easily interpreted and followed. It is not easy.

*Help me to learn your language, to be
at least one small syllable of your love.*

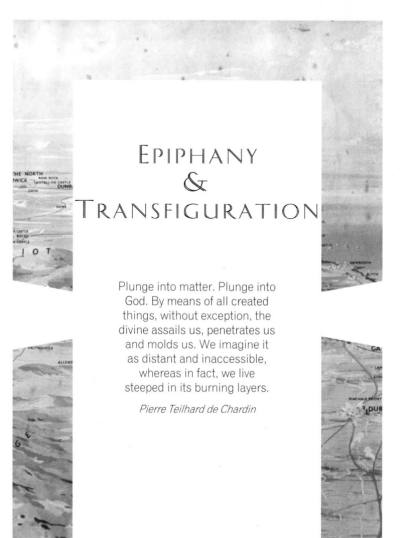

EPIPHANY
&
TRANSFIGURATION

Plunge into matter. Plunge into
God. By means of all created
things, without exception, the
divine assails us, penetrates us
and molds us. We imagine it
as distant and inaccessible,
whereas in fact, we live
steeped in its burning layers.

Pierre Teilhard de Chardin

I Am Not Worthy

Matthew 3:13-17

*I am the one who needs
to be baptized by you. Why
are you coming to me?*

John was reluctant, but Jesus insisted: "Baptize me." John replies, "But I am not worthy. I should be baptized by you."

Do we not often respond the same? "Who am I to do this task, fill these shoes, serve these people? I am not worthy. God needs someone more prepared and qualified, with more training, more experience; someone smarter, kinder, bolder, more humble, less scared, less foolish, less anxious, less *me*."

Stop! Get hold of yourself before that gigantic ego suffocates you! Stop enjoying how amazingly deficient and inadequate you are, and just do what Jesus asks you to do. Wouldn't that be a good closing word in the book of our lives? "She did what Jesus asked her to do." Unworthy even to carry his sandals, but when he asked us to go with him, to be baptized with him, to die with him, we said yes, I am willing. Let it be so. What a testament of devotion to be lowered—humbled, buried—into the waters of love, dying to our private selves and rising into community.

To be baptized, to be initiated into this way of love, is to be given our true name, Beloved of God. Challenges can no longer defeat us, not because we are suddenly competent and unafraid, but because we are no longer our own. We rise from our small selves as offerings, intended for the common good of our world.

*Remind me, again and again, that I do not
need to be worthy. I need only to be yours.*

What Do You Want?

John 1:29-42

Jesus asked them, "What do you want?"
They replied, "Where are you staying?"
Jesus said, "Come and see."

"Look!" John the Baptist calls out. "Here is the Lamb of God who takes away the sin of the world!" How would you like that for an introduction? Not known for his idle small talk, John cuts to the chase: This is the one I've been telling you about. Trust me, I've known him since we were kids. He's the real deal. And he is someone you are going to want to know!

And they do. In fact, two leave John's group to follow Jesus right then and there, which leads Jesus to ask, "What do you want?" They reply, "Where are you staying?" And Jesus answers, "Come and see." Haven't some of our own friendships and adventures started just as oddly as this and ended up just as life-changing?

"What do you want?" is what you could call a loaded question. It can convey impatience or be just a shallow inquiry—or it can linger as one of the eternal questions for which no answer will ever be totally found. Some of us meet Jesus, and ourselves, while pursuing this very question: *What do I want, really?*

Whatever words are used, one thing we all want is the same. We want to learn what love is, and how love gets embodied. "Come and see" is the generous reply. Join me on the journey. Explore your soul's longing. Follow this trail of surrender. Come alongside and get to know Life, your own and the One who is.

Help me to love the questions that
you love, and to come alongside.

Embracing Our Own Call

Matthew 4:12-23

From then on, Jesus
began to preach,
"Turn...turn...turn to God."

Jesus loops his message into John's and then steps out more fully to embrace his own calling. We all have experienced times when, in order to be a faithful follower, we know we must be willing to lead. The only authentic way forward is to claim our own way. It is time to "sound our call" and see if others join us.

This is how it happened for Jesus: He sees a couple of guys fishing—a normal day, like any other. Jesus calls out to them, "Hey, how about casting those nets aside and we go fish instead for *people*?" Regular comedian, eh? Believe it or not, they say, sure, why not! Just like that, they drop their nets, leave their boat—along with their bewildered father—and take off with this fellow Jesus.

You have to think that even Jesus might have been surprised. Maybe he had been musing about it for a while, how much we are driven by our hungers, and how much effort we put into feeding physical hunger while starving for spiritual food. Even so, he surely would not have expected to haul in a couple of live ones the first time he cast his own net!

What odd idea or inner leading is forming in you? Why not say it out loud, cast in a new direction, gather your team, challenge complacency? What would it take for you to give it a try?

If I turned and heard you calling me right now,
what untried path might you be calling me to?

Blessed Are You

Matthew 5:1-12

Jesus sat down to teach them
and said, You are blessed in
surprising ways. Be very glad!

Do not read this passage of scripture. Pray it instead. Let the words and phrases gently enter your heart and mind, like a slow IV drip of healing wisdom. Let go of old interpretations. Expect something new to be given.

Blessing is God's nature. Not anonymously and impersonally, but uniquely. Let it in. *You* are blessed, *each* of us is blessed, with exactly what we need, at exactly the right time. The Creator of the universe is personally and genuinely interested in each part of creation and initiates loving action on our behalf, caring for each of us so greatly.

God loves to love you and me—not by healing our neediness, ridding us of all pain, but by being with us in our pain.

Blessed are you when, even through the cloud of your pain, you are able to see how love gazes upon you. Let how hurt and needy you are, how grieved you are, how lowly and meek you are, how hungry and thirsty for justice you are, how mocked and demoralized you are, let these be the source of all comfort.

Welcome them as the windows through which to see love. Be happy! Be very glad! This way of seeing *is* the realm of heaven, right here, now, among us.

Thank you for making me for blessing—
not to have blessing but to be blessing.

Becoming Salt and Light

Matthew 5:13-20

Even the smallest detail
of God's law will remain until
its purpose is achieved.

Salt and light go mostly unnoticed in the world. Like all the smallest blessings—toenails and lady bugs and eyelashes and sand—they serve us quietly, not straining for significance or position. Yet what a difference they make, simply by being true to their nature, heeding their unique callings and purposes.

We are like them, Jesus says, as ordinary as salt, drawing out the flavors of the world, melting the ice of despair, preserving the fruits of the spirit. We are light, with the ability to warm cold hearts and expose a way through the darkness. We are not meant for hiding; we are meant to be rays of compassion, beams of justice, in these dark-and-darkening days. Get that basket off your head! Shine!

What values are being brought to life through you? Do you and your community shine faithfully the light of love into the darkness? Have you kept your saltiness or have you grown a bit bland and bitter over the years?

We must be protectors of the ordinary. The Light of the World and the Salt of the Earth are within us and among us and conveyed through our actions. When we are true to our essence, we alter the world around us just by being who we are—simply salt, simply light, now.

Help me not to strive to be more than I am but
like you, to be just myself, as simple as that.

Straight Talk

Matthew 5:21-37

You have heard the words
of Moses...but I say....
Your word is enough.

Jesus says he does not cancel the law of Moses; he brings it to fulfillment. What we have interpreted as literal injunctions are misunderstood, unless they are held within the total law of love. In the law of love, Jesus says, anger is just as evil as murder. Calling someone an idiot (or any of the names we call ourselves) is the same as murder. Don't go to God's altar, Jesus says, dragging the weight of this kind of attitude. First be reconciled and then come to God, free.

The same with adultery—the law of love says it is not the act of laying hands on another, but even the thought of laying hands on another, that causes harm. And divorce? You shall not simply hand over a letter and be rid of whatever or whoever annoys you; take responsibility for the long-term effects. Also, stop swearing "by this and by that." Learn to say what you mean, quietly and sincerely. Say "yes" when the answer is *yes*. Say "no" when it is *no*. It really can be as clear and simple as this.

How much less anxious we would be if this kind of straight talk, and straight living, became the norm. With whom do we need to be reconciled? Whom have we annihilated or used for our own selfish pleasure? Words and actions carry weight; they can strengthen us or defeat us, lead us astray or guide us home.

Help me be true to the spirit of your law by being
true in my relationships, with others and myself.

Revenge or Love?

Matthew 5:38-48

You have heard that getting
even is the way of justice,
but I say, don't resist evil.

Which do you enjoy more? Getting even, or loving those who hurt you? We may have heard rumors of love, but getting even is what we have been taught. Stand your ground; don't be a wimp; demand respect; fight for the right; defend your honor.

Jesus shines a light on our misperceptions. He sees the fullness of God's real law, the law beneath the law, the law of love. "You have heard, 'An eye for an eye; a tooth for a tooth.' BUT I SAY, if you are slapped, turn your other cheek to be slapped, too. If you lose your shirt in court, give your coat, too. If a soldier forces you to walk a mile carrying his gear, double it. You have heard, 'Love your neighbor and hate your enemy,' BUT I SAY, keep things simple—love them both."

Will we let Jesus have his say? Do we believe he speaks truth? We might think we do, but then our enemies, outer and inner, sneak up on us, often masquerading as justice. We fall prey to their stern judgments, their icy shame. Can we see through their posturing and love them? Can we fully love ourselves? Take an enemy inventory and share it with a trusted friend. In what ways do you feel wronged and imagine getting revenge? How do you plot against yourself? How have you acted as enemy to another? Do not let your confessor go easy on you. Insist that he or she hold you to God's highest standard, the standard of love.

Forgive me for being so quick to blame
and so very slow to love, to love, to love.

Only Jesus

Matthew 17:1-9

"Get up," Jesus said.
"Don't be afraid." And when they
looked, they saw only Jesus.

We are filled, to the brim and overflowing, with so very many endeavors, striving to please and achieve and earn our place, that it is rare to see "only Jesus." We see our successes, our failures, how much still needs to be accomplished. But only Jesus? Even in the stillness of prayer, we see in our mind's eye people's needs, piles of work to be done, chores to be finished, books to be read, appointments to be kept—but we do not often see "only Jesus."

Experiment during your normal activities. Try doing the tasks of your day—cleaning up, buying food, riding the bus, walking in your neighborhood—with an eye out for Jesus. Read the newspaper with one goal in mind: to see only Jesus. Do reports of wars and refugees and homeless families and disagreements in Congress and empty food pantries and the distress of immigrants and those suffering in prison show us Jesus?

With regular practice, we can train our inner eye to "see only Jesus" in the most ordinary encounters. We can begin to see a bright cloud of communion shining over each encounter, over all the Earth, our precious, hurting home. Once we see this way, we will be unable ever to turn away. Even when facing loss or wrestling with despair, our hearts will know to kneel in wonder. We will begin to be never afraid again.

Only you can teach me your perspective on
the world. Show me each day what you see.

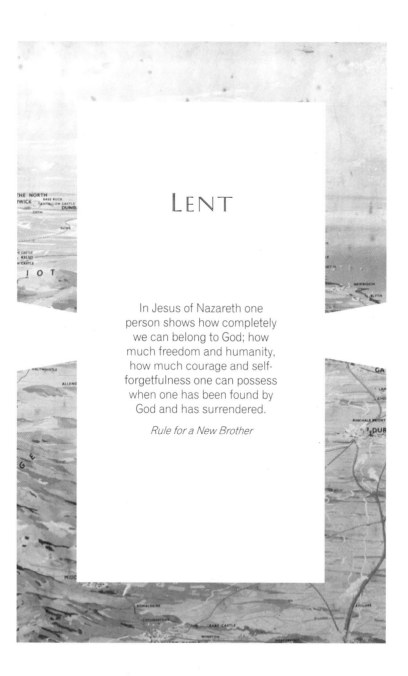

LENT

In Jesus of Nazareth one
person shows how completely
we can belong to God; how
much freedom and humanity,
how much courage and self-
forgetfulness one can possess
when one has been found by
God and has surrendered.

Rule for a New Brother

Do More, Be More, Have More

Matthew 4:1-11

Jesus was led out into
the wilderness by the Holy Spirit
to be tempted there.

Right after his glorious confirmation, right after being assured of his place and purpose—"This is my beloved, in whom I am well pleased"—Jesus faces the wilderness. Great assurance, followed by great difficulty. Is it possible we heard wrong our calling? Have we strayed from the path? Surely God does not mean for the way to be so challenging to follow.

We are called to love and serve our neighbor, and at our best we long to rise to the challenges, to transform all the spaces we inhabit into places to practice love. We want to imagine ourselves as among those who (usually) say *yes* faithfully. Yet here we are, abandoned again in the wilderness. Nothing seems to go smoothly. The money does not flow to support our efforts. People do not embrace us. Healing mercies do not pour through us. The labor is unending and the rewards are scarce. Should it not be easier to walk in the light of love?

We imagine lighter loads that would be more satisfying and sure. Other job descriptions promise success and power and plenty. We imagine basking in appreciation and achievement. We succumb to the temptation to do more, be more, have more. Wilderness strips us down and reveals our true motivations. Temptation clarifies our intention to keep first things first. Love God, love one another, love God, love one another, love God.

Tempt me away from doing, being or
having anything that keeps me from you.

To Know What We Do Not Know

John 3:1-17

In the dark, a religious
leader, a Pharisee,
came to speak to Jesus.

Nicodemus is a courageous man, an intelligent man, a man of good heart, who seeks Jesus under cover of night, asking questions, admitting he does not know what he does not know. What a gift it is when a religious leader can be this humble and curious and willing to learn. Would that we all could more easily admit to being in the dark, admit that we do not understand the life of the Spirit, even while we earnestly seek greater wisdom.

To know what it is that we do not know is the beginning of real knowledge. To admit we do not even know fully what we have been trained to know, and to go to the Source in search of understanding, is the beginning of wisdom.

The humility of confessing our ignorance makes true learning possible.

Twice Nicodemus asks Jesus the sweetest question a student can ask a teacher: "What do you mean?" Such a question says, I'm listening. I'm trying. I don't understand yet, but I sincerely want to learn and grow and discover. Teach me.

Acting as though we already know all we need to know closes doors. An open mind and an open heart, even in the dark, yield understanding.

Teach me to be at home in the dark,
to be at ease with what I don't know.

Only a Woman at a Well

John 4:5-42

Jesus, tired from the long walk,
sat wearily beside the well
when a Samaritan woman came.

Jesus was simply thirsty and tired when he sat down at the well. Maybe in the same way that Rosa Parks was simply tired when she sat down on that bus. Tired physically, and also tired of the injustice and indignity of people being treated as second class citizens of the human race. They were thirsty for new waters of the Spirit to gush forth. At Jacob's well, on a Montgomery bus—like all the ordinary places and ordinary moments of our lives—transformation comes over time *and* occurs suddenly. The eyes of our heart fly open and we see, really see, who sits and stands beside us.

Rosa and Jesus and the anonymous Samaritan woman break free from the carefully constructed boxes of culture and ethnicity and shame, boxes that had been built to keep them imprisoned, and they change their world. Through one unknown, outcast woman in Samaria, people all over the region come to belief in Jesus—not *despite* everything he knows about her and all she has done, but *because* he knows about her, and loves her anyway.

Consider this period of your life. Are you tired? Sit down. Are you thirsty? Ask for something to drink. Who knows how God might want to use even your own weary life to spread the news that love and forgiveness are in our midst.

Help me to be who I am, how I am, where I am,
with whom I am, ever alert for you in the midst.

BLIND ENOUGH TO SEE

John 9:1-41

Why was this man born blind?
Was it sin? Or so that the
power of God will be seen?

Sin, Jesus says, is not the cause of this man's blindness. No, his blindness has a purpose all its own. Even the inability to see, to understand, to be enlightened, can be a gift. Our limitations give God the opportunity to prove the power that is beyond human power. Through the things we perceive as weakness, God's kind of power becomes visible. Because of one man's blindness, many others will see.

Do you believe it, that every part of our lives has holy purpose? Our skills and capabilities, yes, good enough, but even our diminishments and disappointments, our failures and losses? These, too, are gifts? We joke that maybe we serve best by being for others a bad example, a warning. But what if our limitations and failures indeed are intended as blessing? What if to be healed is to be restored not only physically, but in renewed perspectives, deeper understanding, expanded empathy?

"While I am still here in the world," Jesus says, "I am the light of the world." May it be so even now! Shine upon us and through us in our blindness. Restore our sight. Make us a visionary people, O Light of the World. Draw away the curtain of night and shine on us your dawn. Make us, in your mercy, a healed and healing people.

What new depths of perception do you wish
to give, if only I will trust you with my blindness?

Sickness and Sadness Happen

John 11:1-45

*For your sake, I am glad
I wasn't there; this will give you
another opportunity to believe.*

Sickness happens, and sometimes sickness leads to death. This is not how we want life to go. We prefer life, and then more life, and then even more life still, please. We want whatever is good and pleasing to increase daily, hourly, moment by moment—blessed multiplication!

Is this not what God intends for us as well? Has not Jesus promised us abundance? Is this not why we are his friends, the one who is the resurrection and the life? But the truth is, even for friends of Jesus, death strikes close to home, and Martha wants more from her friend than, "Your brother will rise again." She wants to hear Jesus say, "Your brother did not die at all."

We want what we want right now, and we want what we *wanted*, too. We want not only a different present, but a different past. Change our now, Jesus, and then change our future, and while you're at it, reach back and change all that has come before.

Jesus does not chastise Martha for her foolish request. He does not say, "What is done is done; move on." He simply loves her. He weeps with her, weaving her grief into his own. Loss and grief come, yes, but these do not get the final word. They are rolled away, in the fierce solidarity of his love.

*The losses add up and grief grows. Weep
with me, Jesus, then turn me back toward life.*

The Longest Journey

Matthew 26:14-27:66

*"How much will you pay me
to betray Jesus to you?"
"Tonight all of you will desert me."*

What a privilege to walk with Jesus toward his great suffering, and what agony to know we will fail. How far will we make it this time? Will we have the courage to sit down at table with him, or will we rush away? At what point will we fall asleep? Will we be the first, or the last, to deny him?

Such a journey as this one requires greater heart than our own. We must draw upon the collective courage of the faithful through the ages who have walked their own paths of sacrifice and devotion for the sake of "thy kingdom come, thy will be done, on earth as in heaven." We cannot climb this hill alone.

We walk with martyrs and saints, pilgrims and prophets whose stories still today shine light on the path. All who have stepped up boldly or stood silently, who have proclaimed NO to the empire of apathy and YES to God's realm of love; NO to the heavy boot of injustice on the backs of the poor and YES to abundance for all with great need; NO to division and hate and YES to the reconciling light.

Even as the sky grows black, even as the long-awaited one is sealed, dead, in a tomb, we say NO, and we say YES. We keep walking, our lamps lit by the sparks flying off torches carried for generations by the brigade of the faithful.

*Thank you for those who keep the path lit.
They help me keep walking with you.*

EASTER
&
PENTECOST

I must see myself so bound in
love as if everything that has
been done has been done for
me. The Love of God makes such
a unity in us that when we see
this unity no one is able to
separate oneself from another.

Julian of Norwich

What Do You See in the Dark?

John 20:1-18

*While it was still dark, Mary came
to the tomb. At first she saw no one...
then angels, a gardener, the Lord!*

Very early in the morning, when the human eye still struggles to see, resurrection comes. While it is still dark, God arises, greets the day and stirs up some new creation. God mixes up a hearty bowl of resurrection light, serving it all around. Will we join this feast of a new day?

While she is still in the dark, without hope, Mary comes to the tomb to search for hope. She comes to confirm the current darkness, and what does she find? Light! Resurrection means that even in the dark, the dark is already absent. Even in grief, if we can see beyond ourselves, comes a suspicious lightness of being. Mary runs to the other disciples, who in turn race to see for themselves this darkness that is suffused with light.

Resurrection reminds us that darkness always contains more light than we immediately are able to see. Once our eyes adjust, we begin to notice, very gradually, what—and who—is really there. What had seemed to be empty is actually filled: angels, a gardener, Jesus.

What if we assume we will find always and only darkness? Might we end up missing the emerging contours of light? What a loss it would be if we resigned ourselves to seeing only loss, if we gave loss a preeminent place and more power than it deserves.

*Help me to see you even in your
absence, and to recognize you when I do.*

Peace Be With You

John 20:19-31

*They were meeting behind locked
doors when suddenly, Jesus was
standing there among them!*

Huddled in fear behind locked doors, the disciples have lost not
only their guide and teacher and friend but their anchor, their
vision, their hope. They have lost their sense of direction in the
storm. Where shall they look now? To whom shall they turn? Is
everything lost?

And suddenly, Jesus is standing among them! Not merely an
apparition, not a memory, but Jesus himself. His hands, his
side, his wounds—his breath—given as earthy evidence of his
life, which has been laid down and now is given back to them
again. The real Jesus meeting the real need of this particular
moment, showing himself to be who he is, now and forever.

In that moment of moments, his dear bright presence once more
among them, what will he say? What will he do? Each word, each
motion bears weight. He holds out his hands, extends himself
to them, and says, "Peace."

In that simple movement, in that singular word, he also says so
much more. Do not be afraid. Do not huddle, knees knocking,
beside the small bonfire of your own imagination. Come out into
the light of resurrection. Leave behind the fear of what others
can do to you. Even death cannot stop love's resurrection vibe,
the movements of grace. Have faith and live!

*Are you really here, when fear imprisons
me and holds me hostage? Show me.*

A Place to Practice Love

Luke 24:13-35

*Jesus took a loaf of bread, blessed it
and broke it, and gave it. Their eyes
opened, and they recognized him.*

Tangible need, added to tangible offerings, can blossom into intangible blessing. We long for this awareness, that when our hearts break open, Jesus is in our midst.

A man on Columbia Road calls out again and again, "I'm hungry!" Busy folks stream past him on their way to the bus and train. I, too, usually hurry by, but on this day the eyes of my heart are open, and I ask if he would like to come with me half a block to the Potter's House, where I will buy him something to eat.

He isn't so sure. His feet hurt; the Potter's House is not in the direction he is going; he prefers different food; probably money would be better. "But the thing is," I say, "the Potter's House is what I have to give." Reluctantly, he walks with me there.

He sits down at the table nearest the door, under the glowing red of Exit. Before I can ask if he wants a cup of coffee, the cup is already there, with cream and sugar on the side. Someone asks if he would like a sandwich, and another, also without a permanent address, comes over just to say hello.

"What kind of place *is* this?" he asks, eyes darting from art to books to food. I hear myself say, "Oh, this? Just a place to practice love." Beneath our separation beats a heart where we are already one. We just need more places to practice.

*Your compassion pulses for us all. Teach
me to be in sync with your heart's rhythm.*

Fullness of Life

John 10:1-10

*My purpose is life in all
its fullness. An abundance
of life is what I bring.*

We get confused along the way about what makes for abundant life. We end up with packed full lives, but not abundant. Lives brimming with urgent assignments, but not abundance. Lives overflowing with possessions, the most beautiful and well-made items, the latest technologies, but not abundance.

Abundance blossoms in spaces left behind when we pare down and peel away layers of accumulation and acquisition, when we throw off the weight of wanting what others have, the heavy blocks of expectation and disappointment, of competition and comparison.

Abundance flourishes in the soil of the calm and uncluttered mind, the spacious outlook, the carefree spirit. We nurture abundance each time we can say, "I need nothing more," and "Let's try a new way," and "I'm going to slow my pace," and "Why don't we sit together in the silence before we decide."

Abundance creeps in through unlocked minds and undefended hearts, bringing her lovely friends, grace and forgiveness, humility and unfailing love, ease with neighbor and enemy. All manner of good accompanies true abundance. All we must do is make space, open the door of our hearts and hang the sign: "You are welcome here."

*The abundant life is not about having
more stuff, is it? Help me loosen my grip.*

Believing What Can't Be Believed

John 14:1-14

But Jesus, we have no idea
where you are going. How
can we go there with you?

Jesus is the Way, even when we do not know the way. Jesus is the Truth, even when we do not know what is true. Jesus is the Life, even when we do not know what real life means.

Thomas and Philip are bluntly honest: You say we know the way, but we do not. We have no idea where you are going or how to get there. *Have* we met the one you call your loving parent? If so, when? Where? We don't know if we know what you mean.

And Jesus accepts their not knowing. This is one of the gifts Jesus gives us, that he does not judge us by what we know or do not know. He does not lean on our understanding, but invites us to lean on his own. It is not our trust that will save us in the end, but his trust, not our ability to have faith, but his own great faithfulness.

We are not abandoned to figure things out on our own. We have an advocate, a tutor, a dependable and brilliant study partner who is committed to us until enlightenment comes. Layer by layer, insight by insight, we gain deeper understanding. Step by step, we come to a faith that is our own. In the gap between doubt and faith, confusion and trust, stands Jesus—believing in us for as long as it takes for us to believe in him.

My small bucket of faith does not hold very
much, but you make the impossible possible.

WHAT ARE WE LOOKING FOR?

John 14:15-21

You cannot receive the
Spirit when you are not
looking for the Spirit.

We cannot find that for which we are not searching. The Holy Spirit does not barge in uninvited, unsought, undesired. We see what we are ready to see.

Seeking and following the Spirit is a spiral dance of many swirls and loops, rising and falling, with intersecting arcs. Seeking happens by following, and following happens when we seek.

Jesus says, those who seek me love me. Those who love me, follow me. Those who seek, love; and I love them and reveal myself to them.

> "How shall you be revealed?"
>   "As love."
> "How shall we find love?"
>   "Seek and you will find."
> "How shall we seek?"
>   "Do what I ask you to do."
> "What do you ask us to do?"
>   "Love."

And so the journey goes—questing, obeying, discovering, pondering and finding—coming to what we love by becoming love, seeking the Spirit of Love that lovingly seeks us.

I have noticed that your wisdom does not
fit into boxes. What a refreshing free-for-all!

That We Might Be One

John 17:1-11

They were always yours,
and you gave them to me.
Everything I have is from you.

In a heartfelt prayer near the end of his earthly sojourn, Jesus talks with God about his closest circle of friends. "They were always yours," he acknowledges, "and you gave them to me.... Now I am departing the world; I am leaving them behind and coming to you. Keep them and care for them—all those you have given me—so that they will be united just as we are."

How loved we are! We have always been God's—not reluctantly allowed into the circle through the prerequisite of crucifixion, but already God's even before Jesus' sacrificial faithfulness. Oh, what marvelous love is this! Jesus says, "They were always yours." And he does not mean just any God's, but the God who loves us so much that we were given for safekeeping to Jesus, who in turn loves us so much that he asks God, in return, to keep us, together with him. Love and care circling around, gathering us into the eternal embrace, freeing us from fear.

Mercy and grace and healing and hope braid together, one wave overlapping into the next, into a forever folding and looping web of Providence. This is simply who God is, this God in whose likeness we have been created. We are safe. So safe that we can reach far beyond ourselves. Shall we not hold all of creation in the same way so that it, too, might become fully free? Having been loved so much, shall we not risk everything for this love?

O God of providential love, and Jesus the proof of
that love, make us one, woven together in unity.

Peace, Breathe, Forgive

John 20:19-23

They were behind locked doors
when suddenly, Jesus was
standing there among them!

Even our finest locks will not be able to keep out an idea whose time has come. There he is—the best idea ever to have sprung from God's imagination—the resurrected one. He does not criticize his friends for choosing fear, for making a home now behind locked doors. He says, "Peace be with you."

He shows them himself, the best gift he can give. His hands, his side, wounded and healing. And then, once more, "Peace be with you," breathing on them the Holy Spirit and giving them the power and authority to forgive.

What is he doing? He is showing us how to live: Open the doors of your mind. Your wounds can be signs of peace; don't be afraid to let others see you. Take a deep breath. Forgive. Take a deep breath. Forgive. Repeat as needed.

A prayer practice, a way-of-life practice, all of us together, again and again, moments rolling into days and days into weeks. Can you hear the quiet descend and the breathing of billions grow calm? Can you sense peace deepening and expanding into the hidden corners of each heart, and forgiveness rolling through all the nations of the world?

Acknowledge one another's wounds. Breathe peace. Forgive.

Your way of peace is simple and doable.
Forgive my reluctance and fear.

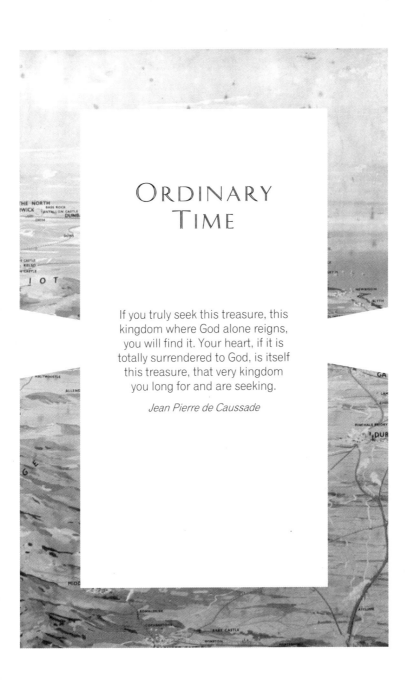

ORDINARY TIME

If you truly seek this treasure, this kingdom where God alone reigns, you will find it. Your heart, if it is totally surrendered to God, is itself this treasure, that very kingdom you long for and are seeking.

Jean Pierre de Caussade

Go and Make Disciples

Matthew 28:16-20

Teach them to obey the
commands I have given
you. I am with you always.

They left again for Galilee, the place where they last had been with Jesus, their familiar home territory—place of miracles and madness, demons and divinity, all the normal stuff of everyday life. Now everything has changed.

Jesus says, "I have been given authority in heaven and on earth." Maybe this is why he could teach us to pray with confidence, "Your kingdom come, your will be done, on earth as in heaven"— because he knew he would be overseeing its completion.

Oh, Jesus, how are we supposed to understand and live this life without you right beside us? How can we know which way to go and what companions to join and how to be who you want us to be? You tell us to make disciples, and we misconstrue your meaning and force a myth about you upon unsuspecting folks. But you are so clear that what it means to be a disciple is simply to choose to follow you, one who never forced yourself upon anyone, but called us always and only to love God and to love our neighbors as ourselves. To love with abandon.

If we can hear what you are asking, and if we can resist the temptation to do it our own way, we will be empowered to come alongside rather than to rule, to be with more than to lord over, and to make disciples by being disciples who are more like you.

Thank you for asking me to
follow you, and not myself alone.

Living in Paradox

Matthew 10:24-39

What I say in the dark, speak
in the daylight. What I
whisper, shout from the roof!

Paradox is not for the simple-minded or faint of heart. Those who know how to dwell only in the architecture of facts will not be at home in the shadowy woods of paradox. Paradox makes different meanings for different people. A certain slant of interior light yields a prism of understandings. With paradox, meaning happens not so much because certain words always mean certain things and always are arranged in certain ways, but because hearer and speaker have a unison of heart and playful spirits and creative minds.

Jesus says there is nothing concealed that will not be disclosed. What is told in the dark will be spoken of in the light, what is whispered in one's ear will be proclaimed from the rooftops. A sword might yield peace, and division might yield unity.

In other words, opposites are not necessarily opposites after all. All things become possible in the upside down kingdom of God's grace. Enemies become friends and our family members might become enemies. Love one another, but not more than you love me. Find your life by losing it; lose your life to find it.

These are not contradictions, but truth, layered. Peel away what you think you already know and discover more than the facts. Discover life's deepest meanings.

You are fond of the poetry of paradox, aren't you?
I see you there, playing between the lines.

Holy Welcome

Matthew 10:40-42

*Anyone who welcomes you
is welcoming me, and welcoming
the One who sent me.*

Do you find it easy to believe that anyone who welcomes you, welcomes Christ? And that anyone you welcome, is welcomed as Christ? In other words, do you believe that *everyone* is included in God's generous welcome and has the power to offer that welcome, or not? All who want to be welcomed, are welcomed. Any who wish not to be welcomed are welcomed.

All who want to be known, and loved anyway, come! All who prefer to be hidden, come! Cornbread for everyone! Falafels all around! Even a cup of cold water, the smallest sort of offering, shared with the smallest sort of person, carries reward. The least for the least yields great blessing. Who are the least? At our best, you are...I am. All who know their need—whether priest or pagan or pauper. All are welcomed.

What joy to be named among the least! To be God's welcomed ones, favored children all. The table keeps expanding and the blessings multiply. This is our central work in Jesus' name—to welcome all who come. To listen and learn from one another, whether of seemingly high status or low, whether sought out or rejected; and to listen and learn from ourselves as well.

How are we doing? Are we on our way to being good hosts for God's kind of holy hospitality?

*Thank you for setting so many places at the
welcome table, and for inviting us to join you there.*

Results Matter

Matthew 11:16-19, 25-30

*I am humble and
gentle, and you will find
rest for your souls.*

"Thank you," Jesus prayed, "for hiding the truth from those who think they are so wise and clever, and for revealing it to the childlike.... For I am humble and gentle, and with me you will find rest for your souls." Striving to appear wise and clever is a favorite competitive sport because it requires absolutely no special abilities. It attracts us because it seems to win us jobs and social status and congratulations. The spoils of the rat race more often go to those thought to be wise and clever than to the humble and gentle.

But who wants the leftovers of a rat? Our lust for power and the false assurances of security and control are so much a part of our common psyche that they are even central themes in our founding story (think tree...temptation...downfall).

Given enough time, education, money, energy, brain and will power, we figure we can know everything we need to know. We can know what to do—and how and when and with whom and why. We can be wise and clever and have significance. We can please God and stun our companions.

But...the truth...will remain...hidden. Why? Because we will not be childlike, innocent and unknowing. We will not be humble and gentle of spirit. We will not have found rest for our souls.

*What I want is hardly ever what I really need,
is it? Help me to stop straining against you.*

Soil Ready and Seed Worthy

Matthew 13:1-9, 18-23

A farmer went out to
plant some seed, and all
manner of results occurred.

God is in the seed-sowing business. That's just who God is. Planting seeds is as common for God as for any farmer. Seeds of new ideas and refreshed traditions, seeds of hope and seeds of forgiveness, common seeds and rare, seeds of longing and seeds of contentment, seeds of controversy, seeds of change— seeds, seeds and more seeds being scattered everywhere! Which ones will take hold and grow? Will the soil receive them? Will we?

Each of us has a part to play in God's seed-sowing, crop-growing business. Sometimes we are given a bag of seeds and sent out to plant them in schools, governments, neighborhoods, cities, churches, even in one another—whether the soil is dried up or fertile. Other times we are handed a hoe and a spade and some blister cream and told to get at it. Break through that hard ground, dig those trenches, prepare the soil for seeds you will never touch but that others one day will bring.

Whether we are called to prepare or to plant, to work or to study or to pray, we can help nurture the kind of soil that will be a good home for seeds. We can devote ourselves to dreaming deep and breaking open and making space for sprouts. We can play our part even if we never see the results.

If you have some seeds that need planting,
I have a spade and a hoe and will give it a go.

On Fire for God

Matthew 13:24-30, 36-43

*The field where the farmer
planted good seed is
now full of weeds!*

All our hard work, ruined. We had prepared the ground, planted the seeds, watered and weeded…and then, invasion. Sometimes among us, sometimes from within us, opposers and naysayers, negativity and judgment, creep in and seek to ruin everything we have been trying to achieve. Should we yank out what seems to be a wicked invader, or simply let all parts grow side by side?

If you ever have tried to eradicate even a disagreeable habit (how *are* those New Year's resolutions coming along?), you know how tough it can be. Focusing on the negative is like shining a sun lamp on it. Oh, how weeds love the light! Besides, who are we to say which are needed for this particular time, this soil—the weeds or the wheat?

Better to do as Jesus says, let them grow side by side. The parts we love alongside whatever we detest. The challenging and the easeful, the dark and the light. Better simply to bend to the task at hand and do what is ours to do. Shower them all with love. Let God tend the fire.

For in the end, so the story says, all will be fire. Whether weeds or wheat, either we will quickly wither or we will blaze forever, like the sun. Will we trust the One who made us to be the One who decides?

*Thank you even for the weeds in my heart,
for all that still awaits fulfillment.*

SMALL AND ORDINARY

Matthew 13:31-33, 44-52

*The smallest of seeds, the most
hidden of treasures, and fish
of every kind reveal God's bounty.*

Small things matter. Simple intentions, brief encounters, little seeds of care planted at the right moment can become the next major thrust or direction for our journey.

We are like that ragged, rugged mustard plant. Viewed from the vista of the whole wide world's pain and joy, we are barely a speck. How can we possibly stand against the world's fierce winds? Yet in our wobbly branches is room for many nests that in turn can provide safe harbor and rest for many small souls.

Treasure abounds in the field of each of us and our small circles. Join in the joy of finding what you did not know you even wanted. Bury it for the fun of finding it again. Did you hear? Something very, very precious is nearby. Dig in, put yourself heart and soul into the search. Take a look into the cracks and crevices you have overlooked before. You never know, you just might find something lustrous shining there.

Like shimmering fish, all kinds, swimming in the waters of your singular life. Cast your net! You won't believe the beauty that gets hauled in. What a wealth of wonders awaits! God plays in the fields of the lowly. Among the small and ordinary, significant treasure can be found. Do you see it? There it is, hidden in plain sight.

*Keep showing yourself to me, hidden right
under my chin. So ordinary, so precious.*

Just Feed Them

Matthew 14:13-21

This is a desolate place and
it is late and people are hungry.
There is no food. "You feed them."

Remember the drug awareness campaign in the 1980's in which addicts were told to "just say no" to drugs? It made addiction sound as though it could be cured through willpower alone, that it is not a complex syndrome with many psychological and physiological barriers. Well-meaning, perhaps, but incomplete.

Jesus, too, sounds as though he might not understand the multifaceted complexity of hunger and poverty when he says to the disciples, "You feed them." What does he expect them to do? How can they provide food for as many as 10,000 to 20,000 hungry people when they have only five small loaves and two puny fish? Doesn't Jesus see that we are limited beings with limited resources? Doesn't he see that we are not God?

Yet Jesus knows we *do* have what we need. If we stop looking only to ourselves, the answer is lying in wait all around us. In the blessing and the breaking of bread, and the power to give it away, casting it like seed to all who are hungry, the gift begins to move, each one to each one, a massive anonymous crowd becoming a communion. Once the sharing begins, don't you see everyone reaching into their baskets to give what they have?

Multiplied generosity, one times two times four, ripples across a sea of need and becomes a feast to feed the world.

Thank you for seeing what I am capable
of being—only human, which is enough.

TELL ME TO COME TO YOU

Matthew 14:22-33

*When Peter saw Jesus on
the water, he called, "If it's
really you, tell me to come."*

Jesus walks on the water toward his friends, so intent is he on being with them. Caught in a sudden squall far away from solid ground, they are frantic with fear. Suddenly Jesus comes toward them. "It's going to be all right!" he calls out. "Don't be afraid."

"If it's really you telling me not to be afraid, Lord, then tell me to come to you," Peter said.

You know the rest. The surge of confidence as he bounds out of the boat and fairly skims across the surface like a speed skier racing toward Jesus, followed by his sudden sinking spell.

We know the Peter phenomenon. All around us, storms rage. Famine and flood bring waves of starvation and disease. Angry winds of partisanship and hate threaten entire systems of government. Isolation and mistrust destabilize neighborhoods. Addiction ravages families. Solid ground is a distant memory, faithful community but a wish dream, when suddenly we think we see him. There he is, calling us to himself.

The key question is, what happens next? May we be given the outrageous audacity to step out into even the most unlikely of places if Jesus is the one calling us. And may we trust ourselves enough to keep trusting him.

*Will you be there if I step out into
the raging waters and come to you?*

Expanding the Table

Matthew 15:10-28

Listen to what I say
and try to understand:
live what you believe.

These two stories seem unrelated:

- Jesus says we are not defiled by what we eat, but by what we say and do. It is not what enters our mouths that matters, but what comes out.

- A woman, consumed with anguish for the well-being of her daughter, argues with Jesus, saying that even outsiders should have a place at the table of God's healing mercy.

On the spot, right then and there, Jesus shows us how to put into practice his own teachings, establishing the efficacy of the truth by embodying the truth. Even more than he might realize, a new order has truly come. No longer are we being judged by religious laws or religious words, but only by an ever-evolving, ever-expanding rule of love in action. The table at which so many legalisms have ruled the day and have kept people separated, becomes now the table of our liberation, a veritable feast of inclusion and healing.

Jesus is saying, don't just talk about your liberation—live it! Embody the revolution that dismantles walls. Disagree for the sake of love. Come, all who hunger for the unity of our God! The table is now ready for all of us.

Even you had to learn by trial and experience,
didn't you, Jesus? Thank you for your humble way.

WHO ARE PEOPLE SAYING I AM?

Matthew 16:13-20

"Who do you say I am?"
"You are the Christ, the son
of the living God."

What a difference it makes if just one person knows who we really are.

We can seek to know ourselves and to be true to ourselves, but if no one else knows us, how unsatisfying self-knowledge is. What we know of ourselves is verified and clarified only in the light of others' responses to us, those who together embody the love of the One who made us. To know ourselves authentically is to see ourselves under the microscope of this magnifying love.

To have a community mirror back to us ourselves, in our sometimes distressing disguises, what an awesome (or might it be awe-full?) gift. What a gift to stand faithfully alongside one another, despite our greatest and our weakest traits, and to stand faithfully with the Jesus who brought us together. And in that circle of light to ask, "Who do you say I am?"

To open our minds and our hearts to whatever answers are given is to be free, free to face our shadows, both dark and bright, to be loved in all our "not yet-ness" and to know who we are and who we are not. "Who do you say I am?" Our willingness to ask this question, as much as the answers that come, will determine the depth of our journey.

Help me to take the risk of getting to
know myself, and letting myself be known.

Understanding a Little or a Lot

Matthew 16:21-28

*If you want to follow me, set
aside selfish ambition, give up
your idea of life, and find life.*

What benefit will it be, to myself or anyone else, if I gain all manner of understanding about the whole wide world, if I learn all there is to know about the religious, cultural, social, governmental, psychological, emotional, logical and illogical workings of life, but stay blind to my soul? Via the wonders of the worldwide web, we now have access to more information than ever before in human history, both vital and ridiculous, uplifting and demeaning, yet we do not seem to grow in wisdom. We do not seem to have more compassion or clearer strategies for living with ourselves or one another in peace.

What *are* the warning signs of a civilization—or a person—moving toward collapse? Despite all our information about Jesus, and all our knowledge about the world, we still crave ambition more than the cross. We put all our efforts into the upward pull rather than the downward path, the way of success rather than sacrifice. We know more than ever about our enemies, except how to love them or lay down our lives for them.

True understanding will come only as we give up our idea of what makes life worthwhile and yield to God's idea. When we surrender the pursuit of our own "best life" in order to disappear into God's best life, we begin to live the only life worth living.

*When I am tempted toward the illusions of
power, disillusion me. Turn me back to you.*

The Simple Way of Community

Matthew 18:15-20

If another sins against you,
here is what to do.... Wherever
two or three of you are, I am there.

Jesus is not a magician dazzling the crowds, performing tricks for their amusement, weaving a gossamer web of lofty and convoluted teachings. No, for Jesus the mystical is grounded in the concrete choices and actions of ordinary life.

When someone in your community offends you (and notice he does not say *if* someone offends you, but *when*), here is what you shall do:

1) Go to the person and try to settle the issue privately;

2) If this does not work, take a couple of others with you;

3) If this does not work, take the issue to the community;

4) If even this effort is unsuccessful, then go all out with the ultra-deluxe package—treat the offender the same as I have told you to treat a pagan or a tax collector.

In other words, treat the offending person as one of your friends whom you love as much as yourself.

There is nothing magical about life together under the rule of love. Just keep widening the circle, going the extra mile, loving your enemy for the sake of unity in diversity. It is as simple, and as difficult, as that.

Life in community would be easy if it weren't for
the people. Help me to love you, right here, right now.

Forgive, and Yet Again, Forgive

Matthew 18:21-35

*Have mercy on others
just as I have mercy on you.
Don't refuse to forgive.*

One thing is clear: we cannot say we follow Jesus while also seeking revenge against our enemies through acts of violence.

Think of the years—not to mention the money, creativity, human lives—we give to the pursuit of revenge that could be spent instead in the pursuit of, not happiness, but forgiveness. What if we devoted years of practice to sharpening our swords of love rather than our weapons of domination? What if we strove to improve our mercy marksmanship rather than raining down enmity on our enemies? What kind of people might we be by now? How truly respected might we be in the world?

Jesus tells a story about servants who borrow money from their king. The one who borrows the most begs to have his debt forgiven, and it is. Do you know what happens next? Does this forgiven one celebrate his good fortune by becoming just as generous and forgiving of all who have ever been indebted to him? Does being forgiven much yield much forgiveness?

Actually, he turns right around and cruelly demands from others what has been forgiven him. Really? Who does that? What is mercy good for if not to reproduce mercy? We learn how to give only by giving, and how to forgive only by forgiving. We still have much to learn.

*I am better at receiving your mercy than giving it.
Forgive me, seventy times seventy times seven.*

Earning a Fair Wage

Matthew 20:1-16

*Heaven is like a day labor
site where the owner agrees
to pay the normal wage to all.*

What do you suppose represents a fair wage at the end of the day? Just enough to feed and house your family? Enough for a college fund or two and maybe a yearly vacation? Whatever amount the other guy is getting, or always a little more? What do you suppose this life you've been living is worth to you?

Have you been living your life? At the end of the day, regardless of when you started, do you deserve the maximum reward? The boss says you do. The boss says better late than never. The boss says good job. You have done enough.

Do you believe it? Do you want to work for such a boss as this, who doles out the same to everyone, the long-time faithful and the new, the full-time worker receiving the same as the temp? Won't the lazy and the diligent both begin to withhold and do no more than the least they can manage? Should someone not be keeping track and reporting in?

Our standard units of measure, our judging and bargaining and trading, are useless here. God lives under a broad banner called Bountiful. Toss out the old ways, the outdated mind. It is time to learn a new currency and a new language. Better to receive what God says we deserve than what we really deserve.

*Help me to trust your accounting, to learn
your language, your customs, your way.*

By Whose Authority?

Matthew 21:23-32

"I won't go," and then he went.
"I will go," and then he did not.
Which one was more obedient?

Who gives us the right to do what we are doing? Or to be who we are being? Does our authority come from heaven or from humans? Are we being obedient with our yes, or with our no? Do our words or our actions matter more?

Questions like these sometimes are simply our avoidance tactics, the way we delay taking our next steps toward the dream of God, at least the part of the dream that is ready to happen through us. Searching for a few more answers to a few more questions helps us delay the pivotal moment of moving out into the unknown and *becoming* the next right answer.

The one with authority is not the one who intends to follow God's instruction, not the one who asks the great questions about God, not the one who reads about God, talks about God, makes big plans for God, but the one who actually stands up and goes.

One son says he will not work in the vineyard, and then does; another says he will work, and then does not. Which one is living his life with authority?

Authority is not earned by diploma or license or acclamation, but by being who we really are and doing what is ours to do. In this way we become the authentic author of our lives. Our wills merge with the One Will, and we live our true authority.

Help me to author my own life, by
living more and more aligned with you.

THE STONE REJECTED

Matthew 21:33-46

The stone once rejected
is now the primary stone.
What a marvel to see!

The way things seem is not always the way things are. What seems unimportant now can become central. What has seemed superior might tumble into a tailspin. Acceptance can bring rejection. What delights us can end up bringing much suffering. Our strongest abilities can create our downfall, and our weakest characteristics might be our saving grace.

We should not be so sure we know how it all will turn out.

What aspects of ourselves, of each other, do we most often reject? What character traits seem unusable, unreliable, irredeemable, null and void? What if the rejected parts are meant to become the cornerstone of our next becoming? Will we have already tossed them out, reduced them to rubble? Will we have imprisoned them in the sub-basement of our souls?

To trust God is to trust the totality of our lives—the complex layers of each of us, and all of us together. The unlovable parts of us have a part to play as much as the admirable; the rejected as much as what has been foundational. Everything belongs.

We are God's partners in creating this holy rearrangement. Rejection is hereby rejected. Restoration now dwells among us.

When I reject myself or anyone else, I risk
rejecting you. Help me to love all of me, all of us.

COME TO THE FEAST

Matthew 22:1-14

*A great feast was all
prepared and ready, but the
guests refused to come!*

Have you shined your dancing shoes? Have you pressed your best clothes and brushed your hair? Are you rested and ready for the royal extravaganza? Choice food has been cooked. The flowers have been delivered. The band is practicing its finest selections. Invitations to one and to all were delivered. All that remains is for you to show up at the party.

How is that part of your story going? *Have* you been showing up lately for the feast of your life?

In this age—less "age of wonder" and more "age of shock and awe"—we have multiple lists of errands to run and things to do, bucket loads of information, but little time to ponder and dream. We have plenty of responsibilities, but no clear sense of call. Activities and relationships, entertaining as they are, fill us to overflowing while our souls starve for nourishment. We receive so many invitations that we end up overlooking the key one, the one inviting us to the Great Feast.

Wouldn't it be a pity if God were trying to throw a party called "your life" and you were too frazzled to attend? Imagine the guest of honor being too busy to show up for the tribute banquet! Which is happening right now, you know. On this very day your presence is requested at a feast in your honor. Your real life awaits. Can't you hear yourself answering, *Yes! Yes! Yes!*

*Thank you for the invitation to the feast
of my life. I can't wait to be here!*

Give God What Is God's

Matthew 22:15-22

They tried to trap Jesus into
saying something for which
they could accuse him.

How simple Jesus' instructions are to all who will listen:
　　Love God.
　　Come home to your true self in me.
　　Do what is yours to do.
　　Give away what God gives to you.
　　Share the good news, each one to each one.

Why do we tend to complicate the simplest of instructions with our scheming? We prefer the game of *What If.* What if this way of being and doing is not adequate for the challenges? What if we end up owing more than we get? What if we give ourselves in the wrong places to the wrong people for the wrong reasons?

Jesus amazes the cynical ones, dismays the critical ones, sets the crooked straight. His ways are easy. Simplify, simplify. Just two easy steps:

1) Give to the rulers what belongs to the rulers;

2) Give to God what is God's.

Who are your rulers? Who is your God? What do you owe each of them? Which one carries the ultimate authority in your life? To which one are you truly devoted?

Why do I tend to complicate my life, when you
have already shown me how simple the way is?

The Most Important Question

Matthew 22:34-46

When the Pharisees heard
he had silenced the Sadducees,
they tried to trap him.

An expert in religious law asks it, the most important question. Not because he truly wants to know, but hoping to trap and ridicule Jesus, he asks: "What is the most important commandment?"

And Jesus, cool and collected, replies with ease: "Love the Lord your God with all your heart, all your soul and all your mind. And equal to this—love your neighbor as yourself. All that ultimately matters is contained here."

Jesus has an important question for them as well: "What about the Messiah—whose son is he?" Is he just trying to change the subject, or does his question get at the heart of the matter?

We can love only those people and ideas with which we have at least some familiarity. We will never be able to love God with our whole selves—our heart, soul and mind—if we do not know who God is. And we will never be able to love our neighbor as ourselves, with good intention and undefended hearts, from our own reserves.

Only if we ourselves discover a connection to the Source of Love will we be able to put into practice God's most important commandments.

Give me the questions I most need right now,
and the answers you most need me to have.

WALKING THE TALK

Matthew 23:1-12

The teachers interpret scripture,
but they do not practice what
they teach. They are of no help.

Jesus says what he means and does what he says. Listen to him. Watch him. You'll see.

Pay attention to your religious teachers, he tells us, and do what they say. But do not—I repeat, DO NOT—follow their example. They might be able to interpret God, but they are not able to implement God.

Here is a better plan. Imagine what the religious teachers would be apt to do, and then do the reverse. Something like this:

- Do not put on a show to impress people.
- Do not take the head seat at a banquet.
- Do not insist on a revered title. Be simply 'brother' and 'sister' to each other.
- Humble yourself; serve one another.

Knowing God's way is a good thing, but knowledge will carry us only so far. Following the leader is a good thing, but leaders can carry us only so far. Embodying God's way, living it together, is all that ultimately sustains.

Be a becoming, not just a knowing.

Do you sometimes wish that I would
quit talking about you and just practice you?

Foolish and Wise

Matthew 25:1-13

*When the bridegroom
was delayed, they all
lay down and slept.*

Everyone fell out of watchfulness and into slumber. *Everyone.*
Whether we are found among the foolish or the wise, none of
us can stay fully alert for the long haul. When we fall into
slumber, we are not alone. And now the really good news: No
one is judged for falling asleep!

In this passage, separation from the feast of God's love comes
not because of the sin of lethargy, dozing off at the most
significant moments. No, the doors lock against us when we
expect others to be prepared and accountable on our behalf,
when we expect to ride in on the coattails of others' goodness
and readiness.

Haven't we sometimes demanded that others be what we are
not? That others live from the depths that we have never
attained? That they be filled with the spirit of love and life even
though that spirit has long ago drained out of us?

Foolishness is not falling asleep, but failing to do my own inner
work. What is foolish is to keep running on empty, and to look
to others for the sustenance that only God can give directly,
each one to each one. There is no admittance to the feast of
love until I learn to care for, to take responsibility for, the flame
of my own life.

*Will I have what I need for the long haul?
Keep me moment by moment, day by day.*

Living in Bounty

Matthew 25:14-30

A man gives money to his
servants to invest for him,
and then calls them to account.

Living in the new realm, the realm of generous accountability, proves harder than we expect. So much has been entrusted to us. How shall we steward the gifts we are being given? Shall we protect and defend them, bury them in the dark cellar of our past failures and disappointments? Shall we put them to work and strive to increase the profit? Shall we hide them or spread them with abandon far and wide?

In other words, shall we leave good enough alone or get busy and produce more? The one who buried his treasure did neither. He did not enjoy the bounty of "enough" nor did he produce more. He chose a common alternative, cowering in fear, afraid of the Giver, afraid of the responsibility of having been entrusted with such an extraordinary gift, afraid of his one agonizingly limited and precious life.

Turning away from life, refusing to risk the joy of becoming—this is what leads to the abyss of outer darkness. Here, where regret and disappointment dwell, is much weeping and gnashing of teeth. Refusing the creative and renewing spirit that longs to find a home within each of us causes the great divide. Each time we banish another of the gifts we have been given, we add to the chasm separating us from the God who is our true home.

Help me to care for and use well the gifts
you have given me. They belong to you.

When Did We See You?

Matthew 25:31-46

When did we see you
hungry and feed you, or
thirsty and give you a drink?

Learning to see is the work of a lifetime.

We scurry from place to place, filled to overflowing with urgency and importance, failing to see those icons of the holy who are in front of us right now. You know the ones I mean—the ones who slow us down, who use long, lumbering sentences without pauses; they smell of wrong opinions and old ideas; they need far more than anyone can give; they show us how far we still live from the land of patient, listening love.

It can be so difficult to truly see, truly hear, truly receive the Christ within each person. Maybe our difficulty is not with the ones we call "hungry" or "thirsty" but with the highly educated and richly blessed, those of superior strength and lofty principles who have been given much yet seem to give back so little. Maybe our difficulty is in accepting and loving ourselves.

We grow blind and deaf to the nature of God in human nature.

Open your mind and your heart. See the one who comes to you in disguise. Receive what is being brought to you through the Christ who dwells in the stranger, through the ways that seem alien, through the love that abides. Drink this cup and live.

Help me to see what I cannot see by myself,
and to be what I cannot be by myself.

KAYLA McCLURG writes The Story, a series of weekly online Gospel reflections at www.inwardoutward.org, where she also manages site content and a daily blog of spiritual quotes. *inward/outward* is a project of The Church of the Saviour in Washington, DC, where Kayla has been a staff member since 1997. She is the point-of-contact for the church's eight faith communities and extended network of ministry organizations. She also facilitates inquiries about the church and manages Andrew's House, a guest house for out-of-town visitors.

This book is the first in a series of three. The other two editions contain meditations on the Gospel passages of Year B and Year C of the Revised Common Lectionary.

Kayla writes a new reflection each week on the Sunday Gospel at www.inwardoutward.org. To receive these via email, sign up for "The Story" by clicking on "Get inward/outward by email" at the bottom of the home page.

You might also be interested in subscribing to "Daily Words," featuring quotes from various authors each Monday through Friday, and "On the Way," occasional reflections from The Church of the Saviour community.